Contents

Phonics Centers
Level D

What's Great About This Book

Centers are a wonderful, fun way for students to practice important skills. The 14 centers in this book are self-contained and portable. Students may work at a table or even on the floor. Once you've made the centers, they're ready to use at any time.

Everything You Need

- Teacher direction page

    How to make the center

    Description of student task

- Full-color materials needed for the center
- Reproducible student activity sheets

Using the Center

The centers are intended for skill practice, not to introduce skills. It is important to model the use of each center before students do the task independently.

Questions to Consider

- Will students select a center, or will you assign the center?
- Will there be a specific block of time for centers, or will the centers be used throughout the day?
- Where will you place the centers for easy access by students?
- What procedure will students use when they need help with the center tasks?
- Where will students store completed work?
- How will you track the tasks and centers completed by each student?

Making an Envelope Center

Materials

- 9" x 12" (23 x 30.5 cm) large envelopes
- scissors
- marking pens
- glue or two-sided tape

Steps to Follow

1. Remove and laminate the center cover page. Glue or tape it to the front of the envelope.

2. Remove and laminate the student direction page. Glue or tape it to the back of the envelope.

3. Remove, laminate, and cut apart the manipulatives (sorting mats, task cards, pockets, etc.) and place them in the envelope.

4. Reproduce the student activity sheet and place copies in the envelope.

Note: If a center contains small pieces such as letter cards, place them in a smaller envelope within the larger envelope.

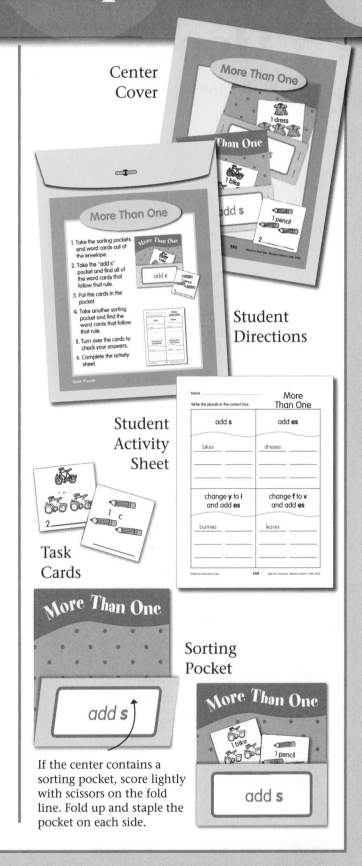

Center Cover

Student Directions

Student Activity Sheet

Task Cards

Sorting Pocket

If the center contains a sorting pocket, score lightly with scissors on the fold line. Fold up and staple the pocket on each side.

Book or Moon?

Skill: Sounds of *oo*

Preparing the Center

1. Prepare an envelope following the directions on page 3.
   Cover—page 5
   Student Directions—page 7
   Sorting Mats—pages 9 and 11
   Word Cards—pages 13 and 15
2. Reproduce a supply of the student activity sheet on page 17.
3. Place all center materials in the envelope.

Using the Center

In a Small Group

Lay the sorting mats (moon and book) faceup on a flat surface. Place the word cards in a small box or bag. Have students take turns choosing a card, reading the word, and listening for the vowel sound. The student then places the card on the correct mat.

Independently

The student sorts and places the word cards on the correct mats. The student then completes the activity sheet by writing the words in the correct box.

Self-Checking Key

Word cards have a moon or a book on the back to match the correct sorting mat.

Book or Moon?

oo in moon

oo in book

roof

wood

noon

6

Book or Moon?

1. Take the moon and book sorting mats and the word cards out of the envelope.

2. As you read the words, listen for the vowel sound.

3. Put the word cards on the correct sorting mats.

4. Turn over the cards to check your answers.

5. Complete the activity sheet.

Skill: Sounds of *oo*

8

oo in moon

9

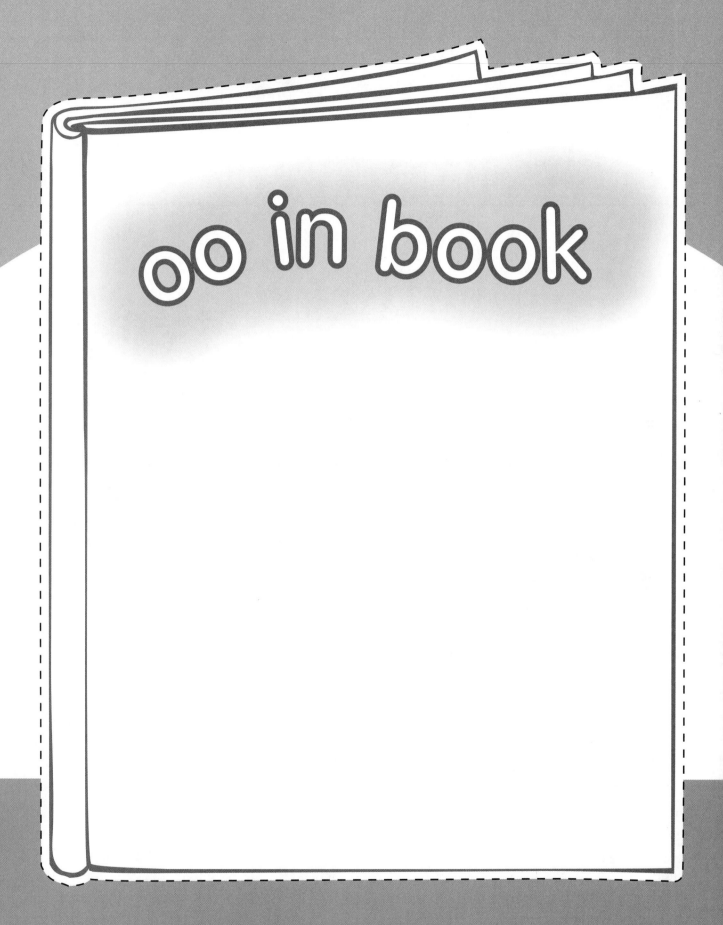

oo in book

11

food	broom	tooth
spool	boot	noon
tool	hoop	roof
goose	zoo	troop

©2004 by Evan-Moor Corp.
Take It to Your Seat
Phonics Centers
EMC 3330

©2004 by Evan-Moor Corp.
Take It to Your Seat
Phonics Centers
EMC 3330

©2004 by Evan-Moor Corp.
Take It to Your Seat
Phonics Centers
EMC 3330

©2004 by Evan-Moor Corp.
Take It to Your Seat
Phonics Centers
EMC 3330

©2004 by Evan-Moor Corp.
Take It to Your Seat
Phonics Centers
EMC 3330

©2004 by Evan-Moor Corp.
Take It to Your Seat
Phonics Centers
EMC 3330

©2004 by Evan-Moor Corp.
Take It to Your Seat
Phonics Centers
EMC 3330

©2004 by Evan-Moor Corp.
Take It to Your Seat
Phonics Centers
EMC 3330

©2004 by Evan-Moor Corp.
Take It to Your Seat
Phonics Centers
EMC 3330

©2004 by Evan-Moor Corp.
Take It to Your Seat
Phonics Centers
EMC 3330

©2004 by Evan-Moor Corp.
Take It to Your Seat
Phonics Centers
EMC 3330

©2004 by Evan-Moor Corp.
Take It to Your Seat
Phonics Centers
EMC 3330

nook	hood	wood
brook	cookies	woof
good	crook	shook
took	stood	hoof

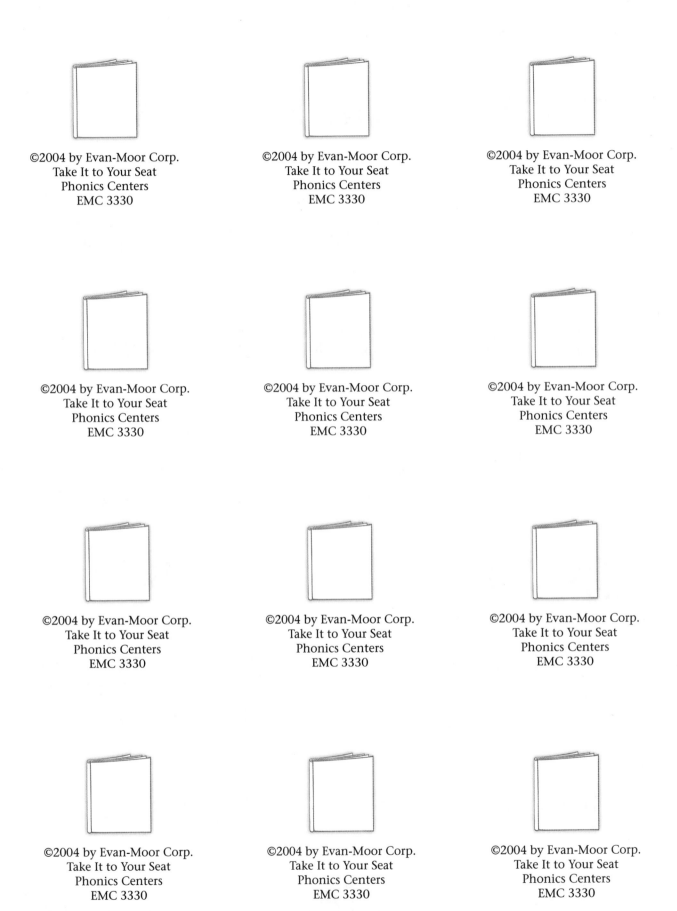

©2004 by Evan-Moor Corp.
Take It to Your Seat
Phonics Centers
EMC 3330

©2004 by Evan-Moor Corp.
Take It to Your Seat
Phonics Centers
EMC 3330

©2004 by Evan-Moor Corp.
Take It to Your Seat
Phonics Centers
EMC 3330

©2004 by Evan-Moor Corp.
Take It to Your Seat
Phonics Centers
EMC 3330

©2004 by Evan-Moor Corp.
Take It to Your Seat
Phonics Centers
EMC 3330

©2004 by Evan-Moor Corp.
Take It to Your Seat
Phonics Centers
EMC 3330

©2004 by Evan-Moor Corp.
Take It to Your Seat
Phonics Centers
EMC 3330

©2004 by Evan-Moor Corp.
Take It to Your Seat
Phonics Centers
EMC 3330

©2004 by Evan-Moor Corp.
Take It to Your Seat
Phonics Centers
EMC 3330

©2004 by Evan-Moor Corp.
Take It to Your Seat
Phonics Centers
EMC 3330

©2004 by Evan-Moor Corp.
Take It to Your Seat
Phonics Centers
EMC 3330

©2004 by Evan-Moor Corp.
Take It to Your Seat
Phonics Centers
EMC 3330

Book or Moon?

Write the words in the correct box.

 **oo** in m**oo**n	 **oo** in b**oo**k
1. _____	1. _____
2. _____	2. _____
3. _____	3. _____
4. _____	4. _____
5. _____	5. _____
6. _____	6. _____
7. _____	7. _____
8. _____	8. _____
9. _____	9. _____
10. _____	10. _____
11. _____	11. _____
12. _____	12. _____

Sound Wheels

Skill: Sounds of *c*, *g*, and *s*

Preparing the Center

1. Prepare an envelope following the directions on page 3.
    Cover—page 19
    Student Directions—page 21
    Sorting Mats—pages 23–27
    Word Cards—pages 29 and 31
2. Reproduce a supply of the student activity sheet on page 33.
3. Place all center materials in the envelope.

Using the Center

In a Small Group
Lay the sorting mats (sound wheels) faceup on a flat surface. Place the word cards in a small box or bag. Have students take turns choosing a card, reading the word, and listening for the highlighted consonant sound. Then the student places the card on the correct mat, in the correct section.

Independently
The student sorts and places the word cards on the correct mats and in the correct sections. The student then completes the activity sheet by reading the words, listening for the highlighted sound, and circling the letter that stands for the sound.

Self-Checking Key
The back of each word card has the letter representing the correct sound.

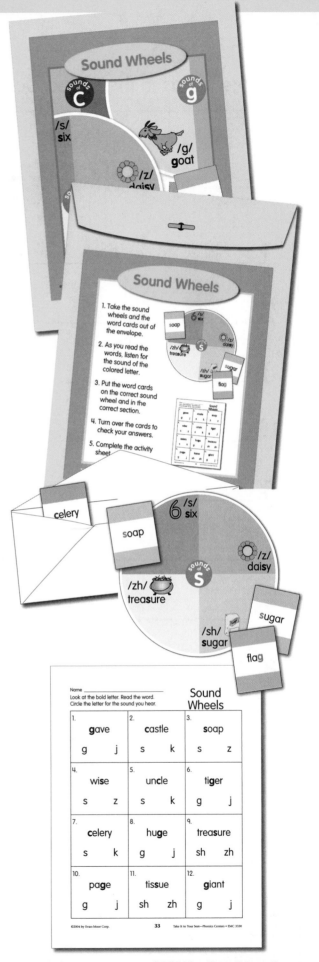

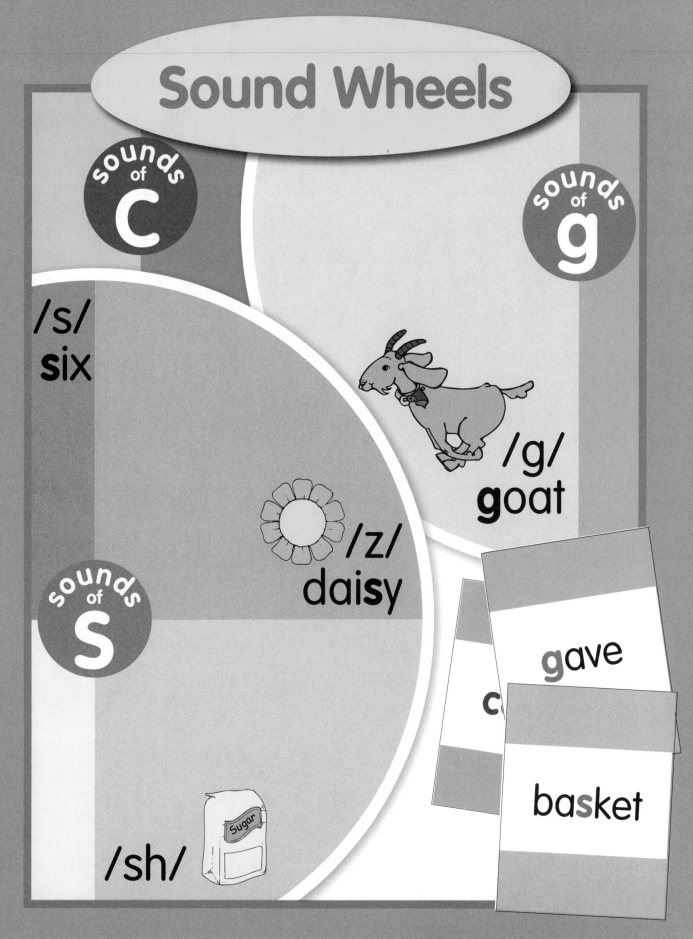

Sound Wheels

sounds of **C**

sounds of **g**

/s/
six

/g/
goat

/z/
daisy

sounds of **S**

/sh/

gave

c...

basket

20

Sound Wheels

1. Take the sound wheels and the word cards out of the envelope.

2. As you read the words, listen for the sound of the colored letter.

3. Put the word cards on the correct sound wheel and in the correct section.

4. Turn over the cards to check your answers.

5. Complete the activity sheet.

Name _____
Look at the bold letter. Read the word.
Circle the letter for the sound you hear.

Sound Wheels

1. **g**ave	2. **c**astle	3. **s**oap
g j	s k	s z
4. wi**s**e	5. un**c**le	6. ti**g**er
s z	s k	g j
7. **c**elery	8. hu**g**e	9. trea**s**ure
s k	g j	sh zh
10. pa**g**e	11. ti**ss**ue	12. **g**iant
g j	sh zh	g j

©2004 by Evan-Moor Corp.   33   Take It to Your Seat—Phonics Centers • EMC 3330

Skill: Sounds of *c*, *g*, and *s*

22

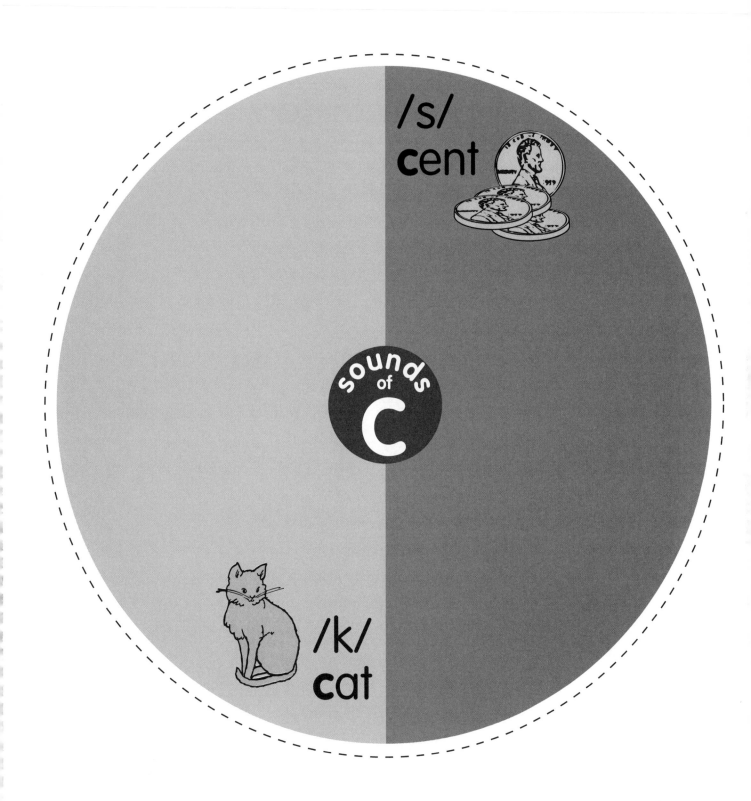

/s/
cent

sounds of C

/k/
cat

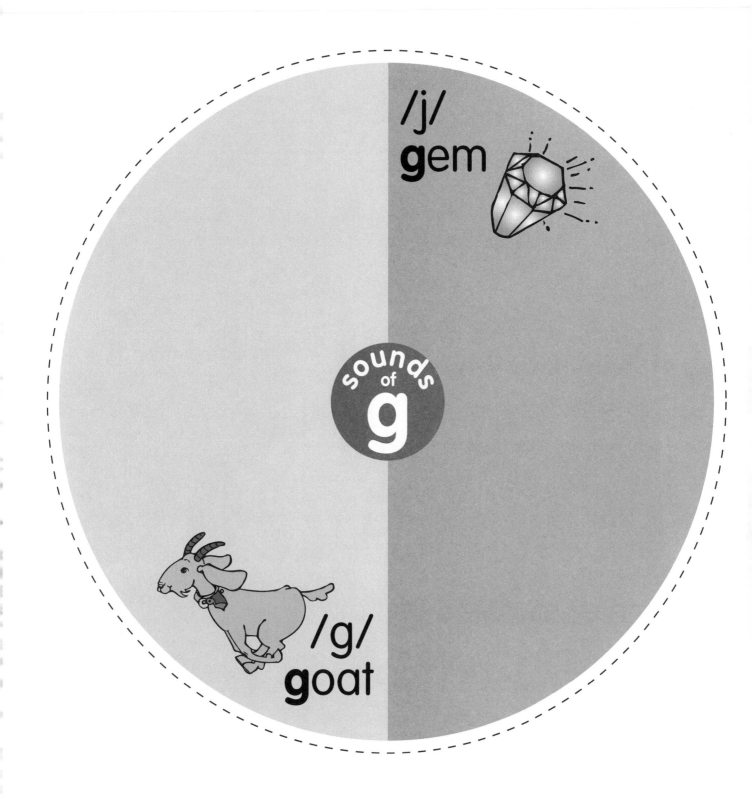

/j/
gem

sounds of g

/g/
goat

26

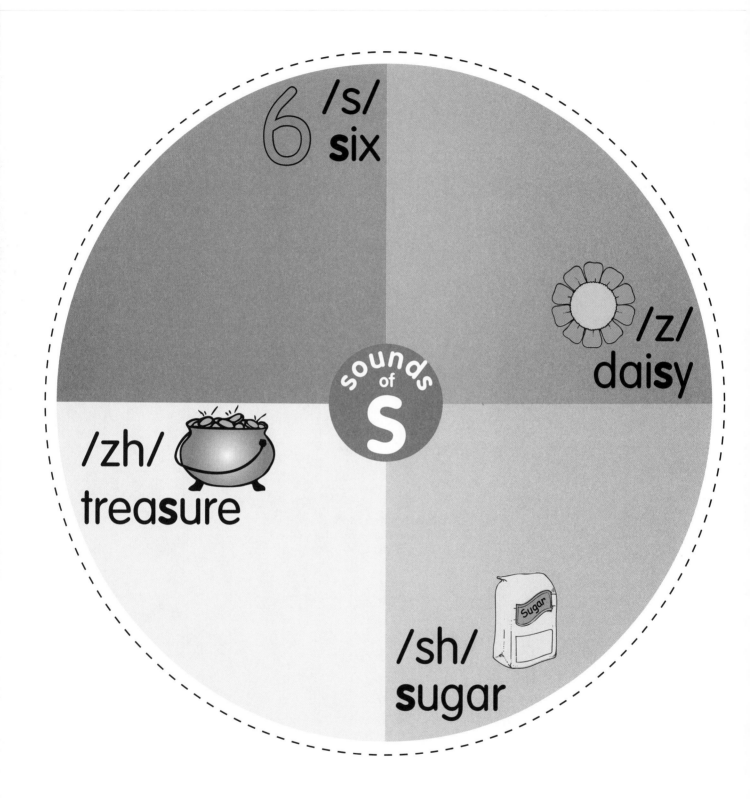

cube	corn	castle	uncle
cent	celery	space	pencil
goose	gave	tiger	flag
giant	giraffe	huge	page

/k/

/k/

/k/

/k/

/s/

/s/

/s/

/s/

/g/

/g/

/g/

/g/

/j/

/j/

/j/

/j/

soap	sock	horse	basket
sugar	sure	tissue	mission
music	busy	wise	please
measure	Asia	television	usual

/s/

/s/

/s/

/s/

/sh/

/sh/

/sh/

/sh/

/z/

/z/

/z/

/z/

/zh/

/zh/

/zh/

/zh/

Name _____

Look at the bold letter. Read the word.
Circle the letter for the sound you hear.

Sound Wheels

1. **g**ave g j	2. **c**astle s k	3. **s**oap s z
4. wi**s**e s z	5. un**c**le s k	6. ti**g**er g j
7. **c**elery s k	8. hu**g**e g j	9. trea**s**ure sh zh
10. pa**g**e g j	11. ti**ss**ue sh zh	12. **g**iant g j

It's a Puzzle

Skill: Sounds of *ch*

Preparing the Center

1. Prepare an envelope following the directions on page 3.
   Cover—page 35
   Student Directions—page 37
   Puzzle Pieces—pages 39–43
2. Reproduce a supply of the student activity sheet on page 45.
3. Place all center materials in the envelope.

Using the Center

In a Small Group

Spread out the puzzle pieces faceup on a flat surface. Place the circular center pieces apart from the rest of the puzzle pieces. Have students take turns choosing and naming a puzzle piece and listening for the sound made by the vowel digraph *ch*. Students place the six pieces for the same digraph sound around the center piece to complete each puzzle.

Independently

The student forms three puzzles, one for each sound represented by the digraph *ch*. The student then circles the letters for the sound made by *ch* in the words on the activity sheet.

Self-Checking Key

Turn over each puzzle. The back of each piece has a dot the same color as the center piece.

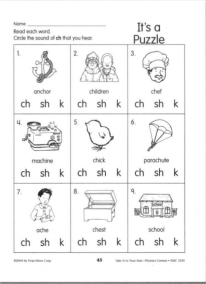

It's a Puzzle

chef

achute

school

School

/ch/

chi

/k/

/sh/

36

It's a Puzzle

1. Take the puzzle pieces out of the envelope.

2. Place the circle pieces to the side.

3. Read the words on the puzzle pieces. Listen for the sound of the letters **ch**.

4. Place the pieces with the correct circle. Keep reading words until you have found all six pieces for one puzzle.

5. Do the other two puzzles.

6. Turn over each puzzle to check your answers.

7. Complete the activity sheet.

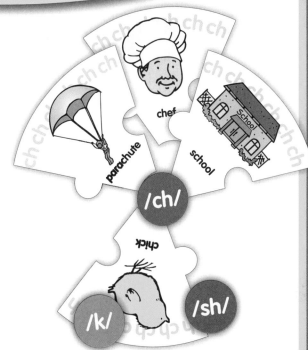

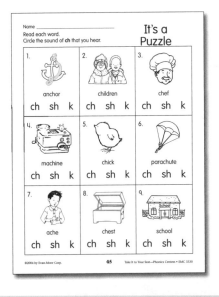

Skill: Sounds of *ch*

38

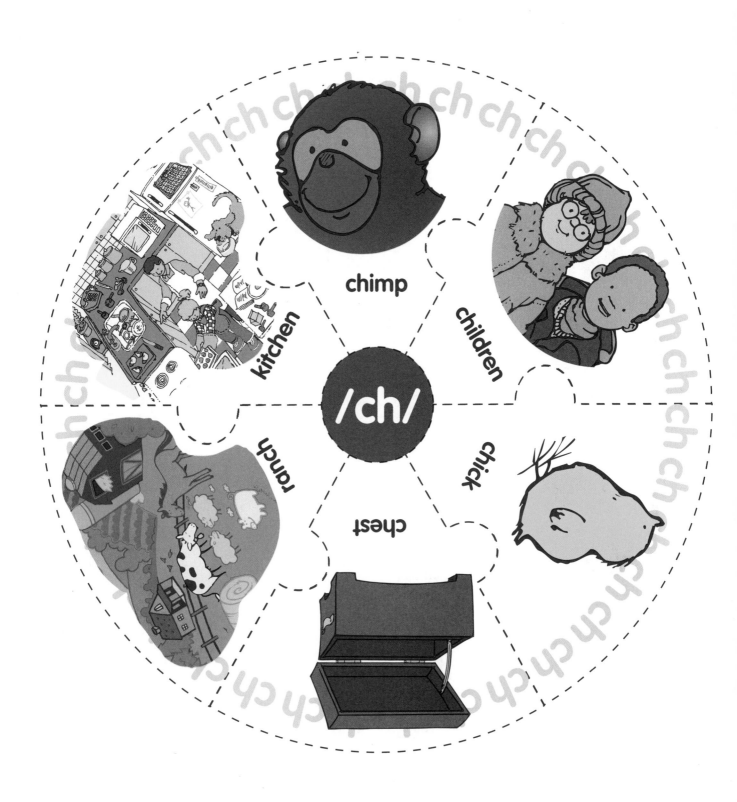

chimp

children

kitchen

/ch/

chick

ranch

chest

©2004 by Evan-Moor Corp.
Take It to Your Seat—Phonics Centers
EMC 3330

©2004 by Evan-Moor Corp.
Take It to Your Seat—Phonics Centers
EMC 3330

©2004 by Evan-Moor Corp.
Take It to Your Seat—Phonics Centers
EMC 3330

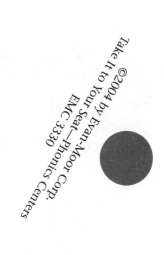

©2004 by Evan-Moor Corp.
Take It to Your Seat—Phonics Centers
EMC 3330

©2004 by Evan-Moor Corp.
Take It to Your Seat—Phonics Centers
EMC 3330

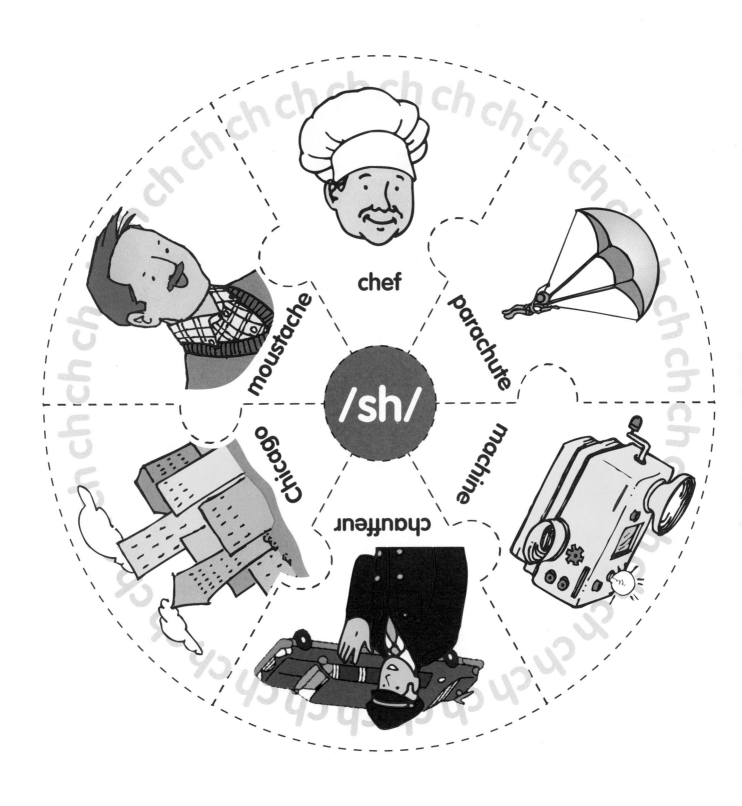

/sh/

chef

parachute

machine

chauffeur

Chicago

moustache

©2004 by Evan-Moor Corp.
Take It to Your Seat—Phonics Centers
EMC 3330

©2004 by Evan-Moor Corp.
Take It to Your Seat—Phonics Centers
EMC 3330

©2004 by Evan-Moor Corp.
Take It to Your Seat—Phonics Centers
EMC 3330

Take It to Your Seat—Phonics Centers
EMC 3330
©2004 by Evan-Moor Corp.

Take It to Your Seat—Phonics Centers
EMC 3330
©2004 by Evan-Moor Corp.

©2004 by Evan-Moor Corp.
Take It to Your Seat—Phonics Centers
EMC 3330

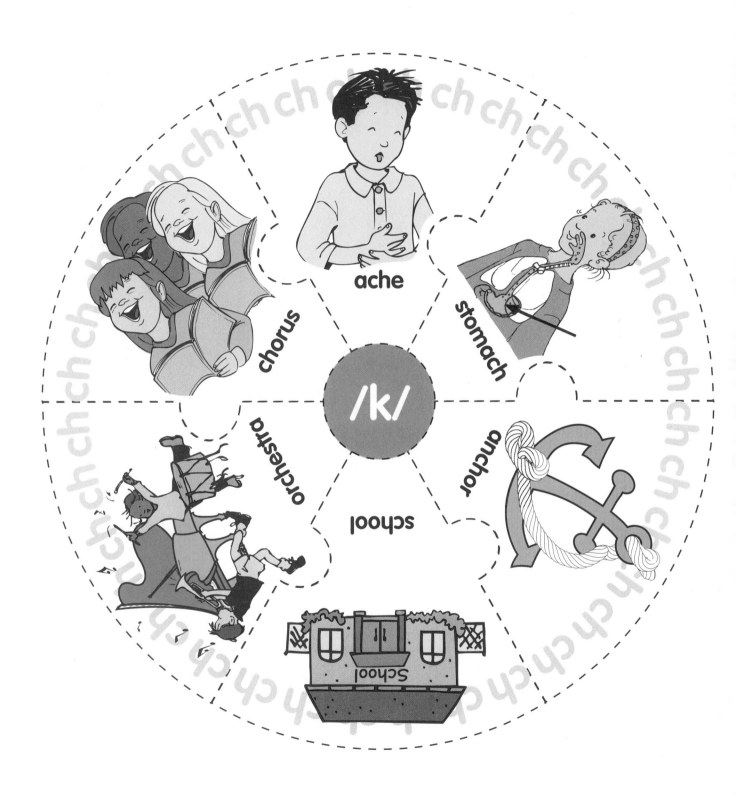

ache

stomach

chorus

/k/

orchestra

school

anchor

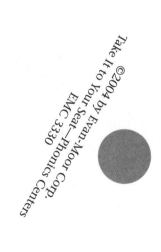

44

Name _____

Read each word.
Circle the sound of **ch** that you hear.

It's a
Puzzle

1.  anchor ch　sh　k	2.  children ch　sh　k	3.  chef ch　sh　k
4.  machine ch　sh　k	5.  chick ch　sh　k	6.  parachute ch　sh　k
7.  ache ch　sh　k	8.  chest ch　sh　k	9.  school ch　sh　k

　45

Then or Thin?

Skill: Voiced/Unvoiced *th*

Preparing the Center

1. Prepare an envelope following the directions on page 3.
   - Cover—page 47
   - Student Directions—page 49
   - Labels—page 51
   - Word Cards—pages 53 and 55
2. Reproduce a supply of the student activity sheet on page 57.
3. Place all center materials in the envelope.

Using the Center

In a Small Group

Place the labels faceup on a flat surface. Read the labels together. Hold up a word card. Have students read the word and decide if the /th/ is voiced as in *then* or unvoiced as in *thin*. Place the card below the correct label. Have students take turns reading a word and determining if they hear the voiced or unvoiced *th*. Continue until all words have been sorted.

Independently

The student sorts the word cards and places them below the correct label according to the voiced or unvoiced *th*.

On the activity sheet, the student fills in the circle in front of *voiced* or *unvoiced* to identify the correct *th* sound in each word.

Self-Checking Key

The back of each word card has a blue or purple shape to match the color of the correct label.

Then or Thin?

unvoiced

/th/ in thin

bath

mother

voiced

/th/ in then

48

Then or Thin?

1. Take the labels and word cards out of the envelope.

2. Listen for the sound of **th** as you read each word.

3. Ask yourself, "Is the **th** sound I hear in **then** or in **thin**?"

4. Place the cards below the correct label.

5. Turn over the cards to check your answers.

6. Complete the activity sheet.

Skill: Voiced/Unvoiced *th*

voiced

/th/ in then

unvoiced

/th/ in thin

52

mother	feather	that
weather	father	this
smooth	they	brother
gather	their	though

53

thumb	**th**imble	**th**irty
thorn	**th**ief	no**th**ing
wi**th**	bir**th**day	ma**th**
think	**th**under	ba**th**

©2004 by Evan-Moor Corp.
Take It to Your Seat
Phonics Centers
EMC 3330

©2004 by Evan-Moor Corp.
Take It to Your Seat
Phonics Centers
EMC 3330

©2004 by Evan-Moor Corp.
Take It to Your Seat
Phonics Centers
EMC 3330

©2004 by Evan-Moor Corp.
Take It to Your Seat
Phonics Centers
EMC 3330

©2004 by Evan-Moor Corp.
Take It to Your Seat
Phonics Centers
EMC 3330

©2004 by Evan-Moor Corp.
Take It to Your Seat
Phonics Centers
EMC 3330

©2004 by Evan-Moor Corp.
Take It to Your Seat
Phonics Centers
EMC 3330

©2004 by Evan-Moor Corp.
Take It to Your Seat
Phonics Centers
EMC 3330

©2004 by Evan-Moor Corp.
Take It to Your Seat
Phonics Centers
EMC 3330

©2004 by Evan-Moor Corp.
Take It to Your Seat
Phonics Centers
EMC 3330

©2004 by Evan-Moor Corp.
Take It to Your Seat
Phonics Centers
EMC 3330

©2004 by Evan-Moor Corp.
Take It to Your Seat
Phonics Centers
EMC 3330

Name _____

Read the word. Fill in the circle to show
if the **th** is voiced or unvoiced.

Then
or Thin?

1. **th**ey ○ voiced ○ unvoiced	2. mo**th**er ○ voiced ○ unvoiced	3. **th**umb ○ voiced ○ unvoiced	4. **th**irty ○ voiced ○ unvoiced
5. ga**th**er ○ voiced ○ unvoiced	6. fea**th**er ○ voiced ○ unvoiced	7. bir**th**day ○ voiced ○ unvoiced	8. ma**th** ○ voiced ○ unvoiced
9. **th**under ○ voiced ○ unvoiced	10. **th**is ○ voiced ○ unvoiced	11. bro**th**er ○ voiced ○ unvoiced	12. too**th** ○ voiced ○ unvoiced
13. **th**orn ○ voiced ○ unvoiced	14. **th**at ○ voiced ○ unvoiced	15. fa**th**er ○ voiced ○ unvoiced	16. wi**th** ○ voiced ○ unvoiced

What's Missing?

Skill: Diphthongs: *oi, oy, ou, ow*

Preparing the Center

1. Prepare an envelope following the directions on page 3.
   - Cover—page 59
   - Student Directions—page 61
   - Picture Cards—pages 63 and 65
   - Letter Cards—page 67
2. Reproduce a supply of the student activity sheet on page 69.
3. Place all center materials in the envelope.

Using the Center

In a Small Group
Lay the picture and letter cards faceup on a flat surface. Hold up one of each diphthong card and ask students to give the sound the letters represent. Next, hold up a picture card. Students name the picture and identify the missing sound in the word. They find the letter card with the correct spelling for that sound and place it on the picture card. Continue the same process with the remaining picture cards.

Independently
The student uses the letter cards to place the missing sounds on each picture card. The student then writes the missing letters to complete the words for each picture on the activity sheet.

Self-Checking Key
The back of each card has the correct spelling of the word.

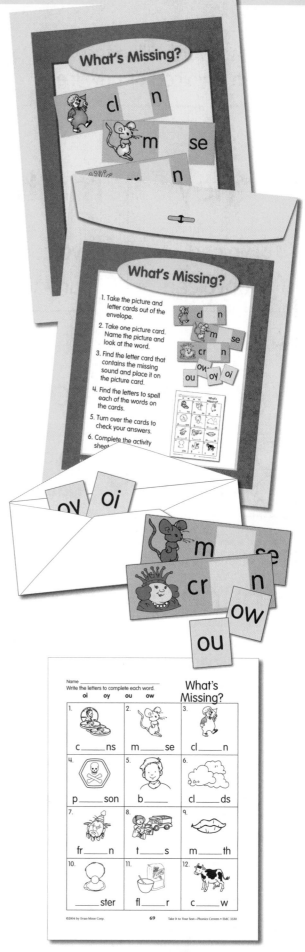

What's Missing?

cl [ ] n

m [ ] se

cr [ ] n

ow

ou

oy

oi

Take It to Your Seat—Phonics Centers • EMC 3330

What's Missing?

1. Take the picture and letter cards out of the envelope.

2. Take one picture card. Name the picture and look at the word.

3. Find the letter card that contains the missing sound and place it on the picture card.

4. Find the letters to spell each of the words on the cards.

5. Turn over the cards to check your answers.

6. Complete the activity sheet.

Skill: Diphthongs: *oi, oy, ou, ow*

62

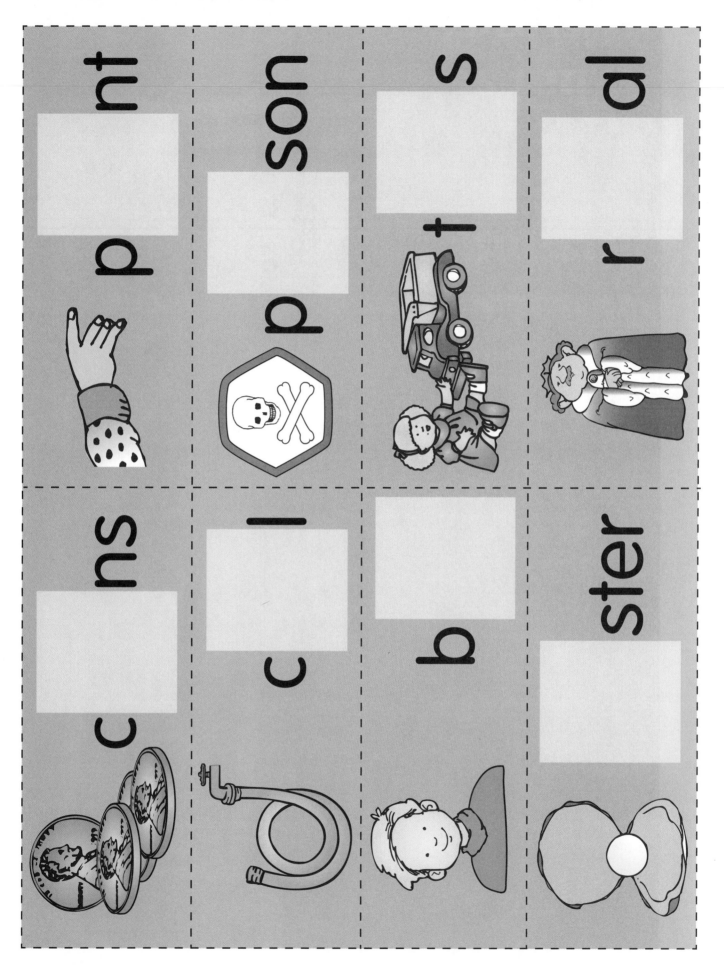

p___nt

___son

p___

___s

r___al

c___ns

c___l

b___

___ster

point

poison

toys

royal

coins

coil

boy

oyster

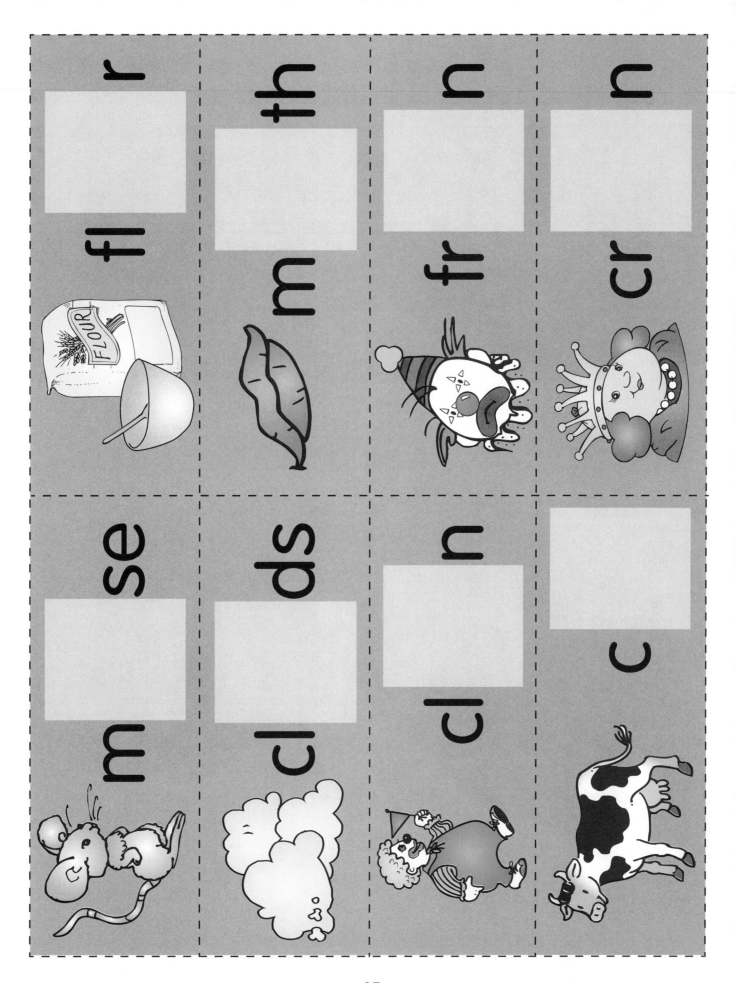

65

flour

mouse

mouth

clouds

frown

clown

crown

cow

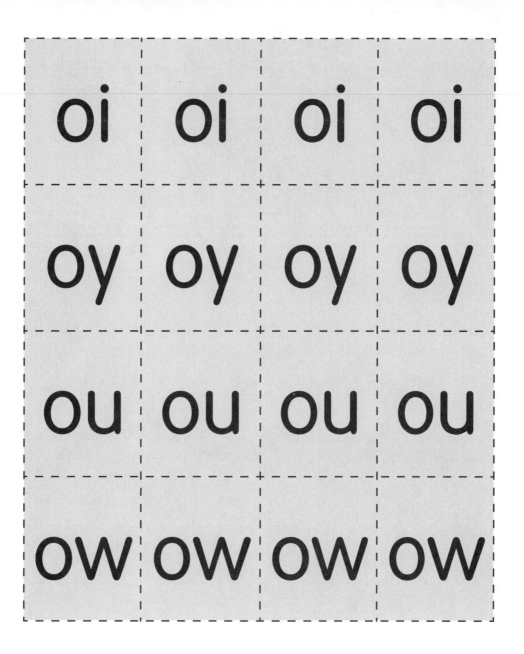

oi	oi	oi	oi
oy	oy	oy	oy
ou	ou	ou	ou
ow	ow	ow	ow

68

Name _____

Write the letters to complete each word.

What's Missing?

oi   oy   ou   ow

1.  c _____ ns	2.  m _____ se	3.  cl _____ n
4.  p _____ son	5.  b _____	6.  cl _____ ds
7.  fr _____ n	8.  t _____ s	9.  m _____ th
10.  _____ ster	11.  fl _____ r	12. c _____ w

Can You Hear It?

Skill: Silent Letters: *b, h, k, n, w, g, c, l, t*

Preparing the Center

1. Prepare an envelope following the directions on page 3.
   - Cover—page 71
   - Student Directions—page 73
   - Sorting Mats—pages 75–79
   - Word Cards—pages 81–85
2. Reproduce a supply of the student activity sheet on page 87.
3. Place all center materials in the envelope.

Using the Center

In a Small Group

Lay the sorting mats faceup on a flat surface. Place the word cards in a small bag or box. Select one card and point out the highlighted letter. Ask students to read the word and listen for the sound of the letter. If they do <u>not</u> hear the sound, place the card on the correct sorting mat in the area labeled *Silent*. If they do hear the sound, place the card on the mat in the area labeled *Not Silent*. Have students take turns choosing word cards until all cards have been placed.

Independently

The student reads the word cards, listens for the sound of the highlighted letter, and then places each card in the correct area of the mat containing that letter. The student copies the words containing silent letters onto the activity sheet and circles the silent letter in each word.

Self-Checking Key

The back of each word card with a silent letter has *s* (for silent).

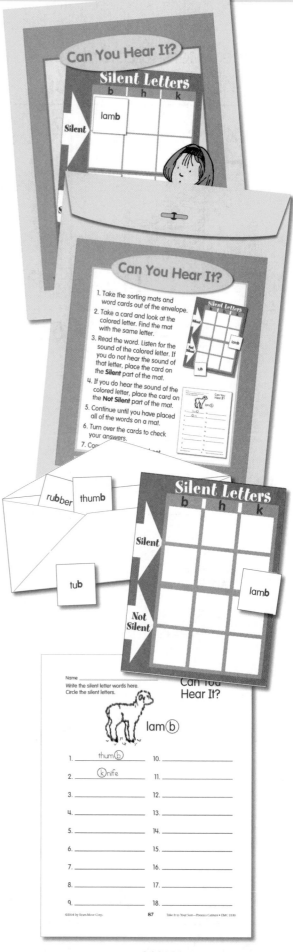

Can You Hear It?

Silent Letters

b	h	k
lamb		

Silent

Not Silent

tub

rubber   **thumb**

72

Can You Hear It?

1. Take the sorting mats and word cards out of the envelope.

2. Take a card and look at the colored letter. Find the mat with the same letter.

3. Read the word. Listen for the sound of the colored letter. If you do <u>not</u> hear the sound of that letter, place the card on the **Silent** part of the mat.

4. If you do hear the sound of the colored letter, place the card on the **Not Silent** part of the mat.

5. Continue until you have placed all of the words on a mat.

6. Turn over the cards to check your answers.

7. Complete the activity sheet.

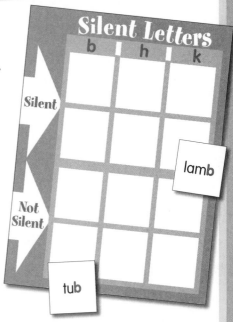

Skill: Silent Letters: *b, h, k, n, w, g, c, l, t*

74

Silent Letters

	b	h	k
Silent			
Not Silent			

76

Silent Letters

	n	w	g
Silent			
Not Silent			

Silent Letters

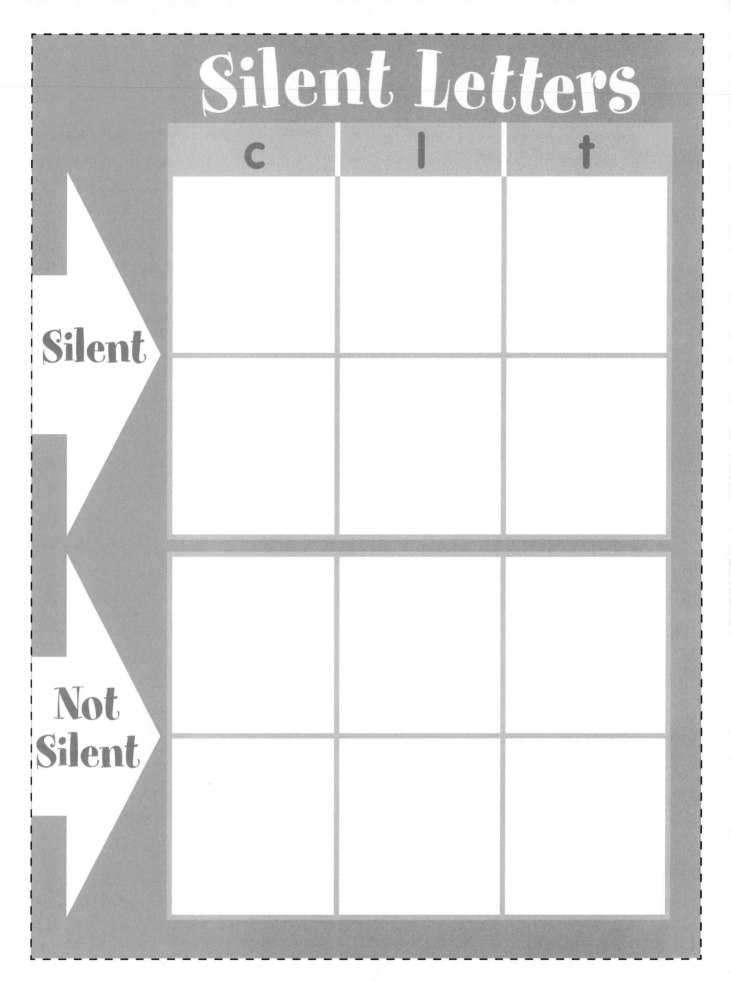

	c	l	t
Silent			
Not Silent			

lam**b**	thum**b**	tu**b**	ru**b**ber
hour	g**h**ost	**h**oney	**h**and
knife	**k**nob	sin**k**	**k**ing

S

S

S

S

S

S

autumn	column	train	nest
wrote	wrong	winter	will
gnaw	sign	garden	goat

S   **S**

S   **S**

S   **S**

scissors	muscle	scare	school
half	talk	hail	list
listen	catch	return	tell

s

s

s

s

s

Name _____

Write the silent letter words here.
Circle the silent letters.

Can You Hear It?

lam(b)

1. _____	10. _____
2. _____	11. _____
3. _____	12. _____
4. _____	13. _____
5. _____	14. _____
6. _____	15. _____
7. _____	16. _____
8. _____	17. _____
9. _____	18. _____

Syllable Count

Skill: 1-, 2-, 3-, 4-Syllable Words

Preparing the Center

1. Prepare an envelope following the directions on page 3.
   - Cover—page 89
   - Student Directions—page 91
   - Sorting Labels—page 93
   - Word Cards—pages 95 and 97
2. Reproduce a supply of the student activity sheet on page 99.
3. Place all center materials in the envelope.

Using the Center

In a Small Group

Lay the sorting labels faceup on a flat surface. Place the word cards in a small bag or box. One at a time, students draw a card and read the word. The group decides how many parts the word contains. *Computer. Computer has three parts. These parts are called syllables.* The student who drew the card places it below the correct label. Students take turns drawing cards until all of them have been placed.

Independently

The student sorts the word cards by number of syllables, placing each card below the correct label. On the activity sheet, the student reads each word and circles the number of syllables it contains.

Self-Checking Key

The back of each word card shows the correct number of syllables in the word.

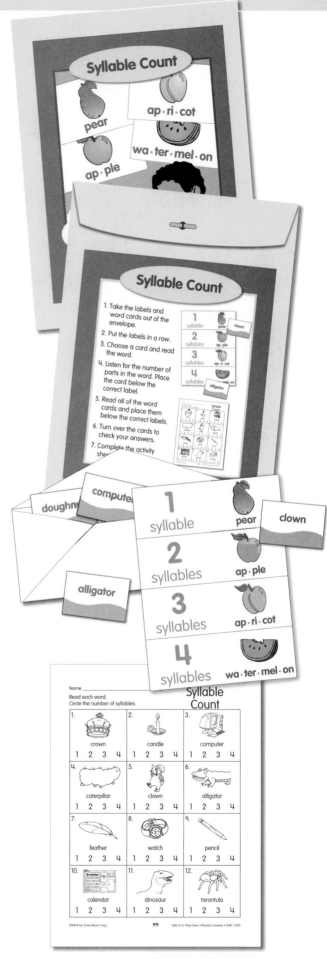

Syllable Count

pear

ap · ri · cot

ap · ple

wa · ter · mel · on

I count 1, 2, 3, and 4 syllables.

90

Syllable Count

1. Take the labels and word cards out of the envelope.

2. Put the labels in a row.

3. Choose a card and read the word.

4. Listen for the number of parts in the word. Place the card below the correct label.

5. Read all of the word cards and place them below the correct labels.

6. Turn over the cards to check your answers.

7. Complete the activity sheet.

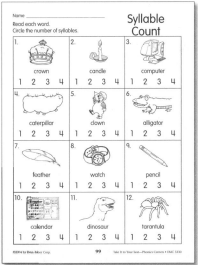

Skill: 1-, 2-, 3-, 4-Syllable Words

Take It to Your Seat—Phonics Centers • EMC 3330

92

1
syllable

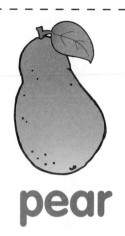

pear

2
syllables

ap · ple

3
syllables

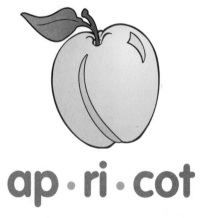

ap · ri · cot

4
syllables

wa · ter · mel · on

clown	throne	swing
smooth	watch	which
rough	through	threw
candle	pencil	feather
ladder	doughnut	fountain
captain	plastic	peanut

Take It to Your Seat—Phonics Centers • EMC 3330

1

©2004 by Evan-Moor Corp.
Take It to Your Seat—Phonics Centers
EMC 3330

1

©2004 by Evan-Moor Corp.
Take It to Your Seat—Phonics Centers
EMC 3330

1

©2004 by Evan-Moor Corp.
Take It to Your Seat—Phonics Centers
EMC 3330

1

©2004 by Evan-Moor Corp.
Take It to Your Seat—Phonics Centers
EMC 3330

1

©2004 by Evan-Moor Corp.
Take It to Your Seat—Phonics Centers
EMC 3330

1

©2004 by Evan-Moor Corp.
Take It to Your Seat—Phonics Centers
EMC 3330

1

©2004 by Evan-Moor Corp.
Take It to Your Seat—Phonics Centers
EMC 3330

1

©2004 by Evan-Moor Corp.
Take It to Your Seat—Phonics Centers
EMC 3330

1

©2004 by Evan-Moor Corp.
Take It to Your Seat—Phonics Centers
EMC 3330

2

©2004 by Evan-Moor Corp.
Take It to Your Seat—Phonics Centers
EMC 3330

2

©2004 by Evan-Moor Corp.
Take It to Your Seat—Phonics Centers
EMC 3330

2

©2004 by Evan-Moor Corp.
Take It to Your Seat—Phonics Centers
EMC 3330

2

©2004 by Evan-Moor Corp.
Take It to Your Seat—Phonics Centers
EMC 3330

2

©2004 by Evan-Moor Corp.
Take It to Your Seat—Phonics Centers
EMC 3330

2

©2004 by Evan-Moor Corp.
Take It to Your Seat—Phonics Centers
EMC 3330

2

©2004 by Evan-Moor Corp.
Take It to Your Seat—Phonics Centers
EMC 3330

2

©2004 by Evan-Moor Corp.
Take It to Your Seat—Phonics Centers
EMC 3330

2

©2004 by Evan-Moor Corp.
Take It to Your Seat—Phonics Centers
EMC 3330

calendar	computer	dinosaur
telephone	wonderful	potato
radio	volcano	parachute
caterpillar	alligator	supermarket
activity	enjoyable	escalator
graduation	kindergarten	tarantula

3

3

3

3

3

3

3

3

3

4

4

4

4

4

4

4

4

4

Name _____

Read each word.
Circle the number of syllables you hear.

Syllable Count

1.	2.	3.

1.

crown

1   2   3   4

2.

candle

1   2   3   4

3.

computer

1   2   3   4

4.

caterpillar

1   2   3   4

5.

clown

1   2   3   4

6.

alligator

1   2   3   4

7.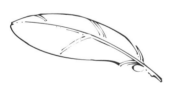

feather

1   2   3   4

8.

watch

1   2   3   4

9.

pencil

1   2   3   4

10.

calendar

1   2   3   4

11.

dinosaur

1   2   3   4

12.

tarantula

1   2   3   4

Can You Spell It?

Skill: Vowel Digraphs

Preparing the Center

1. Prepare an envelope following the directions on page 3.
   Cover—page 101
   Student Directions—page 103
   Word Cards—pages 105–113
2. Reproduce a supply of the student activity sheet on page 115.
3. Place all center materials in the envelope.

Using the Center

In a Small Group

Lay the word cards faceup on a flat surface. Provide an erasable marking pen. Have students take turns choosing a word card, naming the picture, and identifying the vowel digraph that completes the spelling of the word. Circle the correct digraph. Continue until all cards have been completed.

Independently

The student reads each card and decides which digraph is needed to spell the word correctly. The student then writes the word next to the corresponding number on the activity sheet.

Self-Checking Key

The missing digraph is shown on the back of each word card.

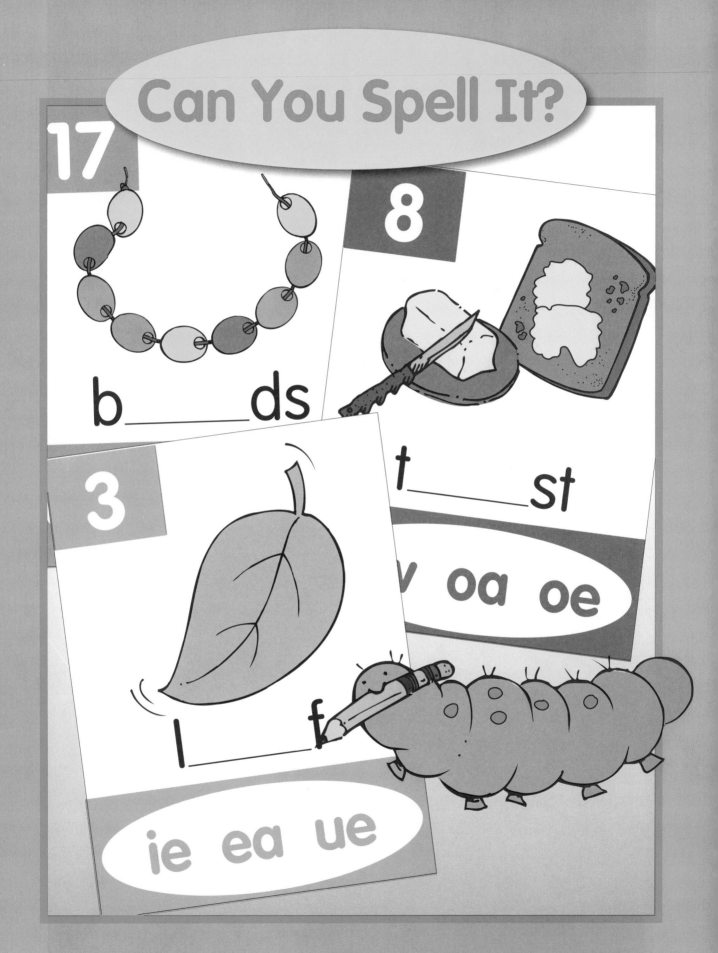

Can You Spell It?

17

b_____ds

8

t_____st

oa oe

3

l_____f

ie ea ue

102

Can You Spell It?

1. Take the word cards out of the envelope.

2. Choose a card and name the picture.

3. Pick the missing letters to correctly spell the word.

4. Pick the letters to spell each of the words on all the other cards.

5. Turn over the cards to check your answers.

6. Complete the activity sheet.

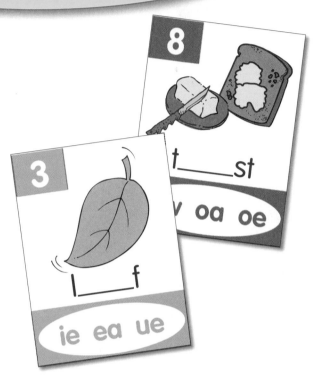

Skill: Vowel Digraphs

1

tr____n

ay ai eigh

2

____t

ay ai eigh

3

l____f

ie ea ue

4

monk____

ie ea ey

 Take It to Your Seat—Phonics Centers • EMC 3330

eigh

ai

ey

ea

5

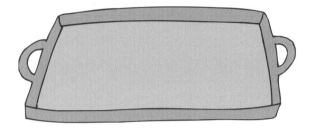

tr_____

ai   ay   eigh

6

p_____

ie   uy   ey

7

b_____

ue   ey   uy

8

t_____st

ow   oa   oe

 Take It to Your Seat—Phonics Centers • EMC 3330

ie

ay

oa

uy

9

b_____l

ow oa oe

10

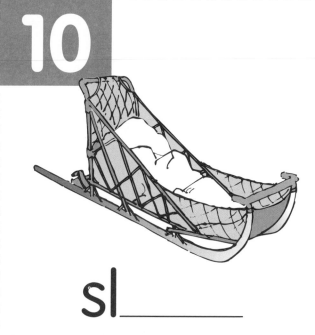

sl_____

eigh ea ai

11

fl_____s

ie ey uy

12

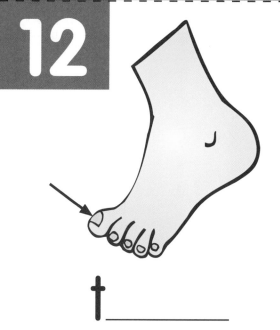

t_____

oa oe ow

eigh

ow

oe

ie

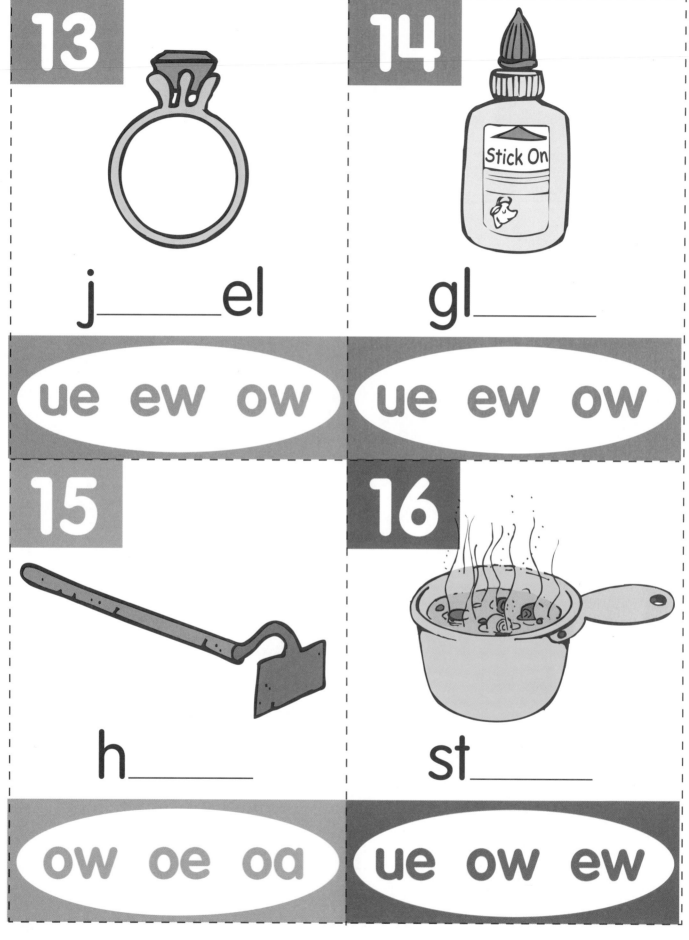

13 j____el

ue ew ow

14 gl____

ue ew ow

15 h____

ow oe oa

16 st____

ue ow ew

Take It to Your Seat—Phonics Centers • EMC 3330

ue

ew

ew

oe

112

17

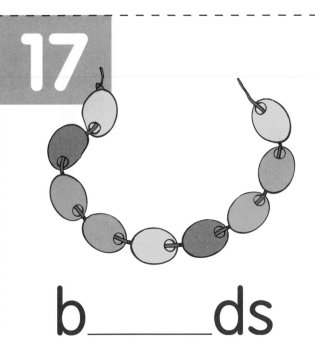

b _____ ds

ey   ue   ea

18

wind _____

oe   oa   ow

19

mon _____

ea   ie   ey

20

bl _____

ew   ue   uy

Take It to Your Seat—Phonics Centers • EMC 3330

ow

ea

ue

ey

Name _____

Can You Spell It?

Write each word next to its card number.

1. <u>train</u>

2. _____

3. _____

4. _____

5. _____

6. _____

7. _____

8. _____

9. _____

10. _____

11. _____

12. _____

13. _____

14. _____

15. _____

16. _____

17. _____

18. _____

19. _____

20. _____

     Take It to Your Seat—Phonics Centers • EMC 3330

Rhyming Riddles

Skill: Rhyming Words

Preparing the Center

1. Prepare an envelope following the directions on page 3.
   - Cover—page 117
   - Student Directions—page 119
   - Riddle Mats—pages 121 and 123
   - Word Cards—page 125
2. Reproduce a supply of the student activity sheet on page 127.
3. Place all center materials in the envelope.

Using the Center

In a Small Group

Lay the riddle mats faceup on a flat surface. Place the word cards in a small bag or box. Select a riddle, read it aloud, and explain that the answer to the riddle is two words that rhyme. Students look through the word cards until they find the answer. *A wet poodle is a soggy doggy*. They place the two words in the boxes on the riddle mat. The group works together to find the correct answer for each riddle. Continue until all riddles have been answered.

Independently

The student uses the word cards to match a two-word rhyming answer to each riddle. The student then writes each correct answer on the activity sheet.

Self-Checking Key

The backs of the two correct word cards have the corresponding riddle number.

Rhyming Riddles

15

a rabbit that
tells jokes

funny

bunny

2

shining sun

bright

light

Rhyming Riddles

1. Take the riddle mats and all of the cards out of the envelope.

2. Read one riddle at a time.

3. Find the two word cards that answer the riddle. Place the cards in the boxes on the riddle mat.

4. Turn over the cards to check your answers.

5. Complete the activity sheet.

Name _____

Rhyming Riddles

Write the answer for each riddle.

1. a toy boa constrictor
2. shining sun
3. a young chicken that is ill
4. a seat for a rabbit
5. a bashful bug
6. an insect doormat
7. home for a small rodent
8. a happy father
9. a colorful vegetable
10. paw warmer for a young cat
11. water bird that wins a prize
12. a wet poodle
13. a fat ape
14. a two-way radio
15. a rabbit that tells jokes
16. a fuzzy fruit
17. a silly flower
18. a skinny horse

©2004 by Evan-Moor Corp.   127   Take It to Your Seat—Phonics Centers • EMC 3330

Skill: Rhyming Words

fake	snake	bright	light
sick	chick	hare	chair
shy	fly	bug	rug
mouse	house	glad	dad
green	bean	kitten	mitten
lucky	ducky	soggy	doggy
chunky	monkey	walkie	talkie
funny	bunny	hairy	berry
crazy	daisy	bony	pony

2	2	1	1
4	4	3	3
6	6	5	5
8	8	7	7
10	10	9	9
12	12	11	11
14	14	13	13
16	16	15	15
18	18	17	17

Rhyming Riddles

Write the answer for each riddle.

1. a toy boa constrictor

_____ _____

2. shining sun

_____ _____

3. a young chicken that is ill

_____ _____

4. a seat for a rabbit

_____ _____

5. a bashful bug

_____ _____

6. an insect doormat

_____ _____

7. home for a small rodent

_____ _____

8. a happy father

_____ _____

9. a colorful vegetable

_____ _____

10. paw warmer for a young cat

_____ _____

11. water bird that wins a prize

_____ _____

12. a wet poodle

_____ _____

13. a fat ape

_____ _____

14. a two-way radio

_____ _____

15. a rabbit that tells jokes

_____ _____

16. a fuzzy fruit

_____ _____

17. a silly flower

_____ _____

18. a skinny horse

_____ _____

Fill It In

Skill: Word Families: *-ead, -ew, -ain, -air*

Preparing the Center

1. Prepare an envelope following the directions on page 3.
   - Cover—page 129
   - Student Directions—page 131
   - Task Cards—pages 133 and 135
2. Reproduce a supply of the student activity sheet on page 137.
3. Place all center materials in the envelope.

Using the Center

In a Small Group

Select one of the sentence cards. Hold up the matching word cards one at a time and call on volunteers to read them aloud. Guide students to realize that all the words end with the same sound. Explain that they are a part of the same word family. Ask students to think of other words that could be a part of the word family.

Read the first sentence aloud. Ask students to determine which of the four word cards best completes the sentence. Repeat the process with each of the remaining sentence cards.

Independently

The student selects one sentence card and the four matching word cards. The student then reads each sentence, selects the word that best completes it, and places the word card in the box.

The student then circles the card color on the activity sheet. He or she writes the words after the correct number. If there is time, the student may select other cards to complete.

Self-Checking Key

The back of each word card indicates the sentence number it completes.

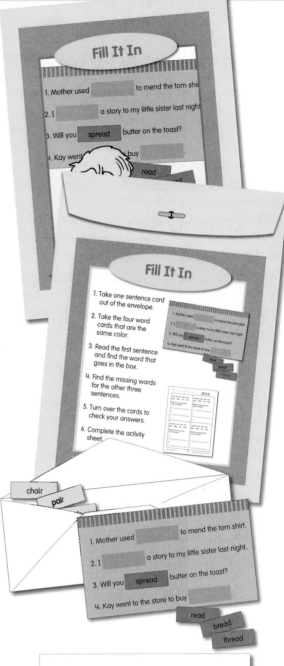

Fill It In

1. Mother used _____ to mend the torn shir[t]

2. I _____ a story to my little sister last night

3. Will you [spread] butter on the toast?

4. Kay went [to] buy _____ .

read

bread

thread

129

130

Fill It In

1. Take one sentence card out of the envelope.

2. Take the four word cards that are the same color.

3. Read the first sentence and find the word that goes in the box.

4. Find the missing words for the other three sentences.

5. Turn over the cards to check your answers.

6. Complete the activity sheet.

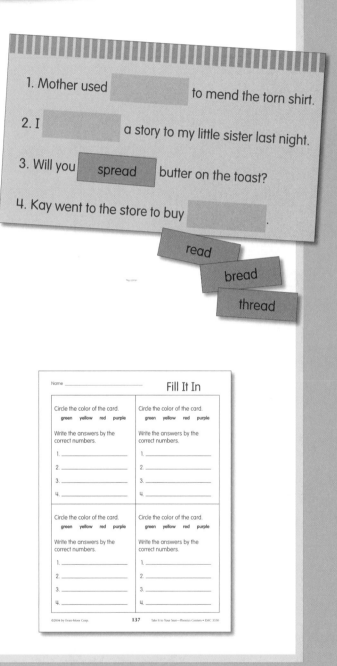

Skill: Word Families: *-ead, -ew, -ain, -air*

132

1. The _____ on her bike broke.

2. It started to _____ just as the game began.

3. Use your _____ when you take a test.

4. Did you _____ your ankle when you fell?

| rain | chain | brain | sprain |

1. Please help me _____ my bike.

2. Sal has a new _____ of shoes.

3. My grandma has a rocking _____.

4. It is _____ to take all of the toys.

| chair | pair | unfair | repair |

4   3   1   2

1   4   2   3

1. Jake [ ] a picture of his dog.

2. She [ ] how to ride a bike.

3. The boys [ ] the ball into the backyard.

4. Drops of [ ] were on the grass this morning.

| dew | drew | threw | knew |

1. Mother used [ ] to mend the torn shirt.

2. I [ ] a story to my little sister last night.

3. Will you [ ] butter on the toast?

4. Kay went to the store to buy [ ].

| read | bread | thread | spread |

2   3   1   4

3   1   4   2

Fill It In

Circle the color of the card.

green   yellow   red   purple

Write the answers by the correct numbers.

1. _____

2. _____

3. _____

4. _____

Circle the color of the card.

green   yellow   red   purple

Write the answers by the correct numbers.

1. _____

2. _____

3. _____

4. _____

Circle the color of the card.

green   yellow   red   purple

Write the answers by the correct numbers.

1. _____

2. _____

3. _____

4. _____

Circle the color of the card.

green   yellow   red   purple

Write the answers by the correct numbers.

1. _____

2. _____

3. _____

4. _____

Word Family Riddles

Skill: Word Families: *-udge, -ight, -ound, -ore*

Preparing the Center

1. Prepare an envelope following the directions on page 3.
   - Cover—page 139
   - Student Directions—page 141
   - Task Cards—pages 143–147
2. Reproduce a supply of the student activity sheet on page 149.
3. Place all center materials in the envelope.

Using the Center

In a Small Group

Have a student choose a riddle card and read the first riddle aloud. Students decide which word card answers the riddle and place it in the box beside the riddle. Continue until all riddles on the card have been answered.

Ask students to look at the word cards to see if they notice anything interesting. Guide them to point out that many of the words rhyme. Explain that these words are part of a word family. Ask students to think of other words that belong in each of the four families. Continue until all four riddle cards have been completed.

Independently

The student selects one riddle card and finds the word cards that answer each of the four riddles. Then the student writes the answers to the riddles in the correct box on the activity sheet.

Self-Checking Key

The back of each word card indicates the number of the riddle it answers in the same color as the corresponding riddle card.

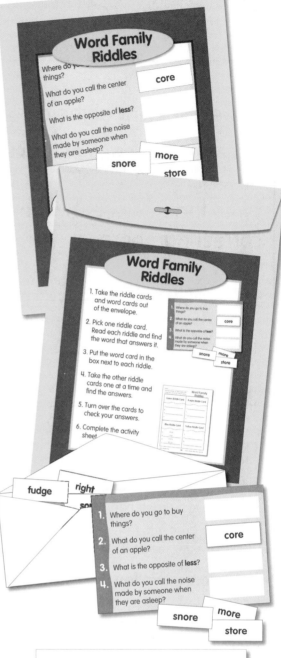

Where do you g... things?

What do you call the center of an apple?

What is the opposite of **less**?

What do you call the noise made by someone when they are asleep?

core

snore

more

store

140

Word Family Riddles

1. Take the riddle cards and word cards out of the envelope.

2. Pick one riddle card. Read each riddle and find the word that answers it.

3. Put the word card in the box next to each riddle.

4. Take the other riddle cards one at a time and find the answers.

5. Turn over the cards to check your answers.

6. Complete the activity sheet.

---

1. Where do you go to buy things?

2. What do you call the center of an apple?

3. What is the opposite of **less**?

4. What do you call the noise made by someone when they are asleep?

core

snore   more

store

Name _____
Write the answer for each riddle in the correct box and by the correct number.

Word Family Riddles

Green Riddle Card	Purple Riddle Card
1. _____	1. _____
2. _____	2. _____
3. _____	3. _____
4. _____	4. _____

Blue Riddle Card	Yellow Riddle Card
1. store	1. _____
2. core	2. _____
3. more	3. _____
4. snore	4. _____

©2004 by Evan-Moor Corp.   149   Take It to Your Seat—Phonics Centers • EMC 3330

Skill: Word Families: *-udge, -ight, -ound, -ore*

142

1. What is dark and sweet and tastes good?

2. Who is the person that picks the winner of a contest?

3. What is a dirty mark made when something is smeared?

4. What do you do when you walk in a tired way?

1. What is the opposite of **wrong**?

2. When you are scared, you have had a _____.

3. Who fights a dragon in fairy tales?

4. What is the opposite of **loose**?

©2004 by Evan-Moor Corp.
Take It to Your Seat—Phonics Centers
EMC 3330

©2004 by Evan-Moor Corp.
Take It to Your Seat—Phonics Centers
EMC 3330

1. Where do you go to buy things?

2. What do you call the center of an apple?

3. What is the opposite of **less**?

4. What do you call the noise made by someone when they are asleep?

1. What is the name for a kind of dog?

2. What do you do when you hit a nail with a hammer?

3. What do you call something you hear?

4. What shape is something that doesn't have corners?

fudge	judge
smudge	trudge
right	fright
knight	tight
store	core
more	snore
hound	pound
sound	round

147

2   1

4   3

2   1

4   3

2   1

4   3

2   1

4   3

Name _____

Write the answer for each riddle in the correct box and by the correct number.

Word Family Riddles

Green Riddle Card

1. _____
2. _____
3. _____
4. _____

Purple Riddle Card

1. _____
2. _____
3. _____
4. _____

Blue Riddle Card

1. _____
2. _____
3. _____
4. _____

Yellow Riddle Card

1. _____
2. _____
3. _____
4. _____

More Than One

Skill: Plurals

Preparing the Center

1. Prepare an envelope folder following the directions on page 3.

      Cover—page 151
      Student Directions—page 153
      Rule Card—page 155
      Sorting Pockets and Word Cards—
          pages 157–163

2. Reproduce a supply of the student activity sheet on page 165.

3. Place all center materials in the envelope.

Using the Center

In a Small Group

Use the rule card to review the rules for writing plurals. Then place the sorting pockets and word cards faceup on a flat surface. Take the sorting pocket for "add s." Ask each student to find a word card that follows that rule. Have students read their card aloud, spell the plural form of the word, and then place the card in the sorting pocket. Repeat these steps with the remaining sorting pockets and cards.

Independently

The student sorts all of the cards and places them in the correct pockets. The student then writes the plural forms of the words in the correct boxes on the activity sheet.

Self-Checking Key

The back of each word card shows the correct plural ending.

More Than One

1 dress

More Than One

1 bike

s

add s

1 pencil

2 _____

152

More Than One

1. Take the sorting pockets and word cards out of the envelope.

2. Take the "add s" pocket and find all of the word cards that follow that rule.

3. Put the cards in the pocket.

4. Take another sorting pocket and find the word cards that follow that rule.

5. Turn over the cards to check your answers.

6. Complete the activity sheet.

Skill: Plurals

154

More Than One
Rule Card

Add **s** to most words.

    cat   cat**s**
    hare   hare**s**

If a word ends in **s**, **ch**, **sh**, **ss**, or **x**, add **es**.

    bus   bus**es**
    beach   beach**es**
    box   box**es**

If a word ends in a **consonant** and **y**, change the **y** to **i** and add **es**.

    cherry   cherr**ies**

If a word ends in **f** or **fe**, change the **f** to **v** and add **es**.

    calf   cal**ves**
    wife   wi**ves**

156

More Than One

1 stamp
2

1 pencil
2

1 bug
3

1 cat
2

1 bike
2

1 coat
3

fold

s pp a

add s

add s

add s

add s

add s

add s

add s

158

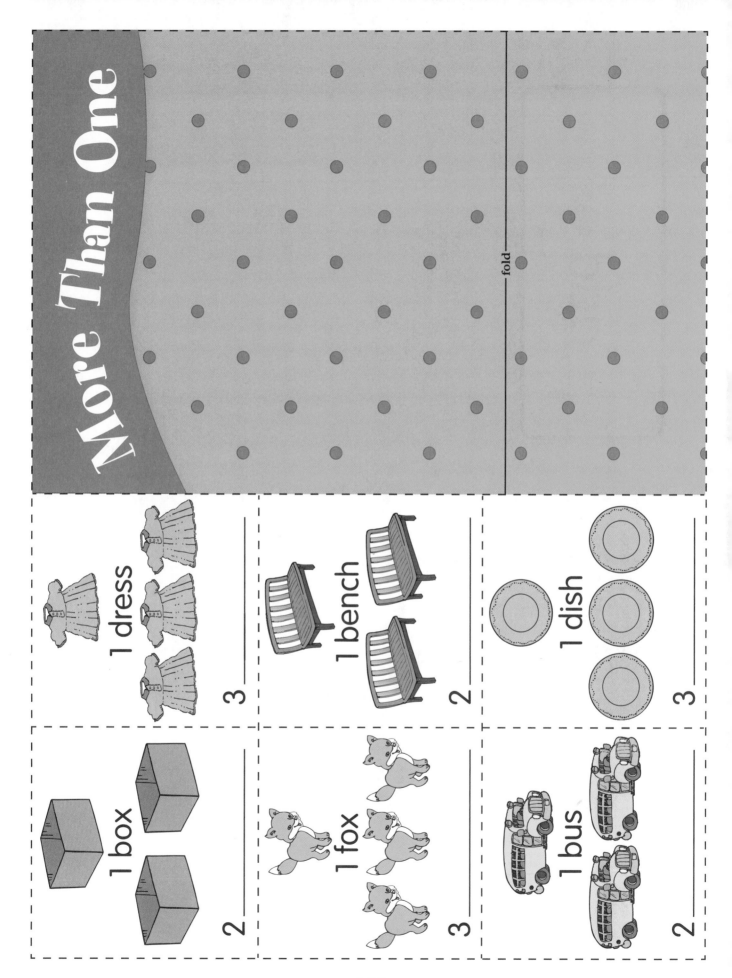

More Than One

1 dress
___
3

1 bench
___
2

1 dish
___
3

1 box
___
2

1 fox
___
3

1 bus
___
2

159

fold

add es

add es

add es

add es

add es

add es

add es

160

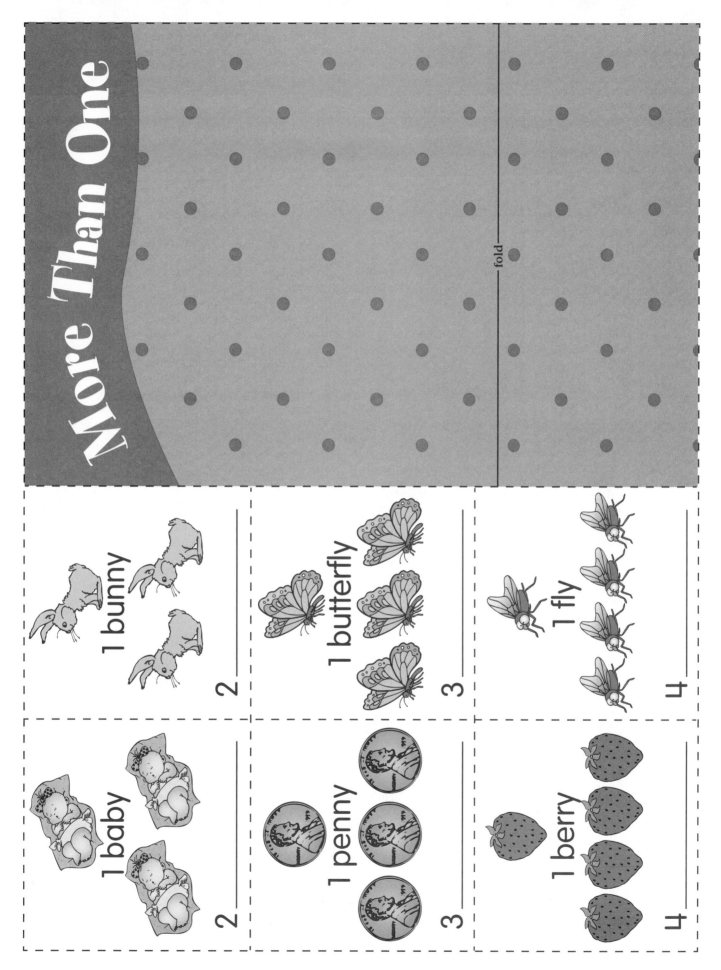

More Than One

1 baby
2

1 bunny
2

1 penny
3

1 butterfly
3

1 berry
4

1 fly
4

fold

change **y** to **i**
and add **es**

y to **i** and
add **es**

y to **i** and
add **es**

y to **i** and
add **es**

y to **i** and
add **es**

y to **i** and
add **es**

y to **i** and
add **es**

162

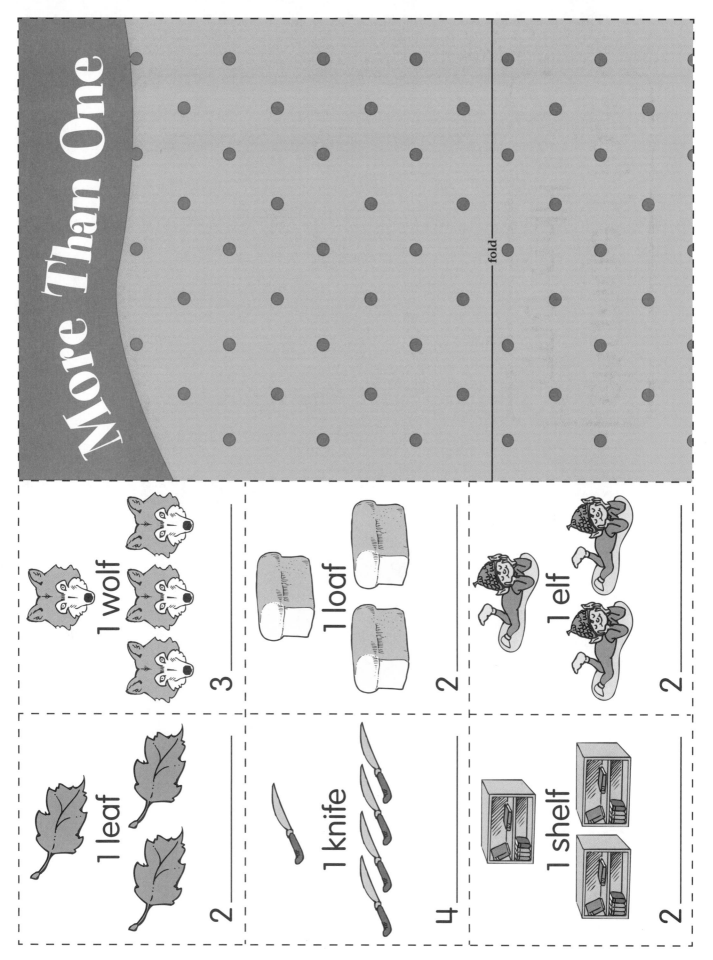

More Than One

fold

1 wolf
3 ___

1 loaf
2 ___

1 elf
2 ___

1 leaf
2 ___

1 knife
4 ___

1 shelf
2 ___

change f to v and add es

f to v and
add es

f to v and
add es

f to v and
add es

f to v and
add es

f to v and
add es

f to v and
add es

f to v and
add es

More Than One

Write the plurals in the correct box.

add **s**	add **es**

change **y** to **i** and add **es**	change **f** to **v** and add **es**

The Right Ending

Skill: Inflectional Endings

Preparing the Center

1. Prepare an envelope following the directions on page 3.
   Cover—page 167
   Student Directions—page 169
   Word Cards—pages 171–175
2. Reproduce a supply of the student activity sheet on page 177.
3. Place all center materials in the envelope. Note: Provide a supply of large paper clips with this center.

Using the Center

In a Small Group

Place one set of cards in a small paper bag or box. Provide a supply of large paper clips. Each student selects a card and uses a paper clip to mark the word on their card that shows the correctly spelled ending. Ask each student to read the directions on the card aloud and then share their answer with the group. *My card says to add ed to walk. The answer is walked, w-a-l-k-e-d.* Continue until all of the cards in each set have been completed.

Independently

The student uses paper clips to mark the words with the correctly spelled endings. The student then completes the activity sheet by adding *ed*, *ing*, and *ly* to words.

Self-Checking Key

The back each card has a star marking the correct answer. The answer is correct if the paper clip is touching the star.

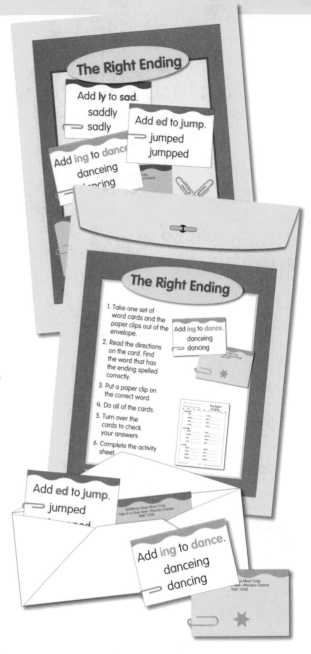

The Right Ending

Add **ly** to **sad**.

saddly

sadly

Add **ed** to **jump**.

jumped

jumpped

Add **ing** to **dance**.

danceing

dancing

©2004 by Evan-Moor Corp.
Take It to Your Seat—Phonics Centers
EMC 3330

by Evan-Moor Corp.
Take It to Your Seat—Phonics Centers
EMC 3330

168

The Right Ending

1. Take one set of word cards and the paper clips out of the envelope.

2. Read the directions on the card. Find the word that has the ending spelled correctly.

3. Put a paper clip on the correct word.

4. Do all of the cards.

5. Turn over the cards to check your answers.

6. Complete the activity sheet.

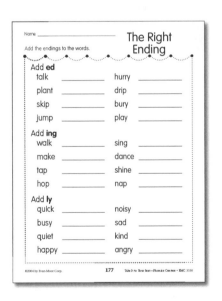

Skill: Inflectional Endings

Add **ed** to **jump**.

jumped

jumpped

Add **ed** to **talk**.

talked

talkied

Add **ed** to **skip**.

skiped

skipped

Add **ed** to **hurry**.

hurryed

hurried

Add **ed** to **drip**.

driped

dripped

Add **ed** to **bury**.

buryed

buried

Add **ed** to **play**.

played

playyed

Add **ed** to **plant**.

planted

plantted

Add **ing** to **walk**.

walking

walkking

Add **ing** to **make**.

making

makeing

Add **ing** to **tap**.

taping

tapping

Add **ing** to **hop**.

hoping

hopping

Add **ing** to **sing**.

singging

singing

Add **ing** to **dance**.

danceing

dancing

Add **ing** to **shine**.

shining

shineing

Add **ing** to **nap**.

napping

naping

Add **ly** to **quick**.

quickly

quickkly

Add **ly** to **busy**.

busily

busyly

Add **ly** to **quiet**.

quietily

quietly

Add **ly** to **happy**.

happly

happily

Add **ly** to **noisy**.

noisly

noisily

Add **ly** to **sad**.

saddly

sadly

Add **ly** to **kind**.

kindly

kinddly

Add **ly** to **angry**.

angrily

angrly

The Right Ending

Add the endings to the words.

Add **ed**

talk	_____	hurry	_____
plant	_____	drip	_____
skip	_____	bury	_____
jump	_____	play	_____

Add **ing**

walk	_____	sing	_____
make	_____	dance	_____
tap	_____	shine	_____
hop	_____	nap	_____

Add **ly**

quick	_____	noisy	_____
busy	_____	sad	_____
quiet	_____	kind	_____
happy	_____	angry	_____

177

Make a New Word

Skill: Prefixes and Suffixes

Preparing the Center

1. Prepare an envelope following the directions on page 3.
   Cover—page 179
   Student Directions—page 181
   Sorting Mats—pages 183 and 185
   Prefix and Suffix Cards—page 187
   Answer Cards—page 189
2. Reproduce a supply of the student activity sheet on page 191.
3. Place all center materials in the envelope.

Using the Center

In a Small Group

Lay the prefix sorting mat and cards faceup on a flat surface. Review the meaning of the prefixes with students. Working together, place the prefix cards in front of the base words to make new words. Ask for volunteers to use each new word correctly in a sentence.

Repeat the steps with the suffix mat and cards. Explain to students that in some cases two different suffixes can be added to a word to make two new words.

Independently

Using either the prefix or suffix sorting mat and cards, the student makes new words. On the activity sheet, the student writes the new words in the correct column. The student repeats the steps with the other cards. Finally, the student writes sentences with two new words.

Self-Checking Key

Cut apart the answer cards on page 189. Place these in a legal-size envelope and place it in the large center envelope.

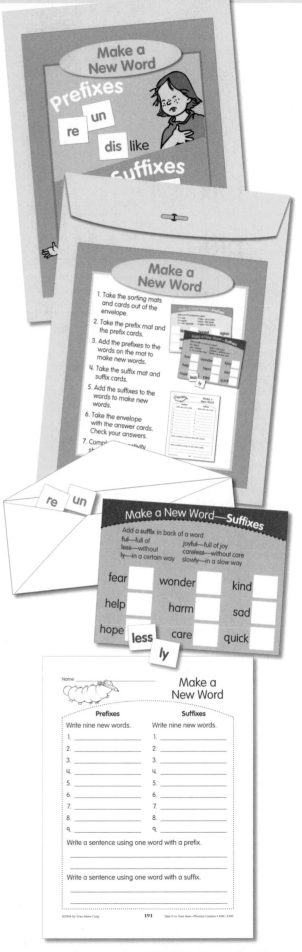

Make a New Word

Prefixes

re un

dis like

Suffixes

less

ly

wonder ful

179

Make a New Word

1. Take the sorting mats and cards out of the envelope.

2. Take the prefix mat and the prefix cards.

3. Add the prefixes to the words on the mat to make new words.

4. Take the suffix mat and suffix cards.

5. Add the suffixes to the words to make new words.

6. Take the envelope with the answer cards. Check your answers.

7. Complete the activity sheet.

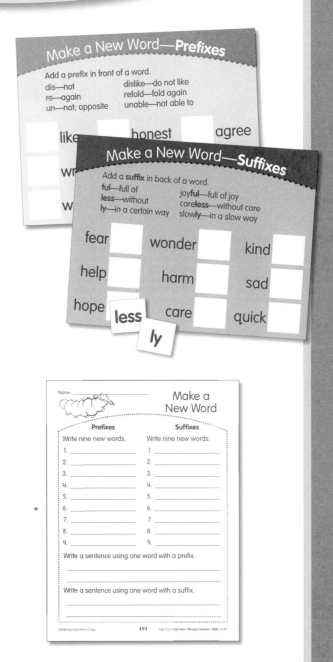

Make a New Word—Prefixes

Add a **prefix** in front of a word.
dis—not   dislike—do not like
re—again   refold—fold again
un—not; opposite unable—not able to

like   honest   agree

wr...

w...

Make a New Word—Suffixes

Add a **suffix** in back of a word.
ful—full of   joyful—full of joy
less—without   careless—without care
ly—in a certain way slowly—in a slow way

fear   wonder   kind

help   harm   sad

hope   care   quick

less

ly

Name ____

Make a New Word

Prefixes	Suffixes
Write nine new words.	Write nine new words.

1. ____
2. ____
3. ____
4. ____
5. ____
6. ____
7. ____
8. ____
9. ____

Write a sentence using one word with a prefix.
____
____

Write a sentence using one word with a suffix.
____
____

©2004 by Evan-Moor Corp.   191   Take It to Your Seat—Phonics Centers • EMC 3330

Skill: Prefixes and Suffixes

182

Make a New Word—*Prefixes*

Add a **prefix** in front of a word.

dis—not

re—again

un—not; opposite

dislike—do not like

refold—fold again

unable—not able to

agree

build

ripe

honest

turn

happy

like

write

wrap

184

Make a New Word—Suffixes

Add a **suffix** in back of a word.

ful—full of   joyful—full of joy
less—without   careless—without care
ly—in a certain way   slowly—in a slow way

kind

sad

quick

wonder

harm

care

fear

help

hope

dis	dis	dis
re	re	re
un	un	un
ful	ful	ful
less	less	less
ly	ly	ly

188

Answers **Prefixes**	Answers **Suffixes**
dislike	fear**ful** or fear**less**
dishonest	wonder**ful**
disagree	kind**less** or kind**ly**
rewrite	hope**ful** or hope**less**
return	harm**ful** or harm**less**
rebuild	sad**ly**
unwrap or **re**wrap	hope**ful** or hope**less**
unhappy	care**ful** or care**less**
unripe	quick**ly**

Make a New Word

Prefixes	**Suffixes**

Write nine new words. Write nine new words.

1. _____ 1. _____

2. _____ 2. _____

3. _____ 3. _____

4. _____ 4. _____

5. _____ 5. _____

6. _____ 6. _____

7. _____ 7. _____

8. _____ 8. _____

9. _____ 9. _____

Write a sentence using one word with a prefix.

_____

_____

Write a sentence using one word with a suffix.

_____

_____

Answer Key

Take It to Your Seat—Phonics Centers • EMC 3330

Page 17
(Order of words will vary.)
moon:
food
broom
tooth
spool
boot
noon
tool
hoop
roof
goose
zoo
troop

book:
nook
hood
wood
brook
cookies
woof
good
crook
shook
took
stood
hoof

Page 33
1. g
2. k
3. s
4. z
5. k
6. g
7. s
8. j
9. zh
10. j
11. sh
12. j

Page 45
1. k
2. ch
3. sh
4. sh
5. ch
6. sh
7. k
8. ch
9. k

Page 57
1. voiced
2. voiced
3. unvoiced
4. unvoiced
5. voiced
6. voiced
7. unvoiced
8. unvoiced
9. unvoiced
10. voiced
11. voiced
12. unvoiced
13. unvoiced
14. voiced
15. voiced
16. unvoiced

Page 69
1. coins
2. mouse
3. clown
4. poison
5. boy
6. clouds
7. frown
8. toys
9. mouth
10. oyster
11. flour
12. cow

Page 87
(Order of words will vary.
Bold letters should be circled.)
lam**b**
thum**b**
hour
ghost
knife
knob
autum**n**
colum**n**
wrote
wrong
gnaw
si**g**n

scissors
muscle
half
talk
listen
catch

Page 99
1. 1
2. 2
3. 3
4. 4
5. 1
6. 4
7. 2
8. 1
9. 2
10. 3
11. 3
12. 4

Page 115
1. train
2. eight
3. leaf
4. monkey
5. tray
6. pie
7. buy
8. toast
9. bowl
10. sleigh
11. flies
12. toe
13. jewel
14. glue
15. hoe
16. stew
17. bead
18. window
19. money
20. blue

Page 127
1. fake snake
2. bright light
3. sick chick
4. hare chair
5. shy fly
6. bug rug
7. mouse house

8. glad dad
9. green bean
10. kitten mitten
11. lucky ducky
12. soggy doggy
13. chunky monkey
14. walkie talkie
15. funny bunny
16. hairy berry
17. crazy daisy
18. bony pony

Page 137
Green
1. chain
2. rain
3. brain
4. sprain

Yellow
1. repair
2. pair
3. chair
4. unfair

Red
1. drew
2. knew
3. threw
4. dew

Purple
1. thread
2. read
3. spread
4. bread

Page 149
Green Riddle Card
1. fudge
2. judge
3. smudge
4. trudge

Purple Riddle Card
1. right
2. fright
3. knight
4. tight